OLD GENT:
A NORWAY SPRUCE

Marie J. S. Phillips

OLD GENT:
A Norway Spruce

ISBN: 978-1-4583-4942-2

Imprint: Lulu.com

9 781458 349422

TABLE OF CONTENTS

<u>DEDICATIONS</u>

To my wonderful husband, Ed Phillips, whose love and support over the decades, proved priceless in my writing career.

To my friend and mentor, Mr. David Ayscue, (November 1953 - September 2010) who proof read my work, and taught me proper punctuation techniques, bequeathing to me an invaluable gift I shall treasure for the rest of my writing life.

To Brothers Tree Service-who help me keep Old Gent's offspring and landmates healthy and vigorous.

And to Old Gent himself, whose grand presence is still missed, almost two decades after his felling.

ONE

Under a bright spring afternoon sun, a young conifer stood, fearful, as humans worked, building a dwelling in the abandoned field where he sprouted a mere decade ago. The humans' tools ended the lives of his fellow trees and shrubs, who fell under the onslaught. The metallic ring and thud of axes filled the field as humans dropped his taller field mates. Wildlife fled in terror. Birds retreated to adjacent lands, twittering and chirping in distress.Humans then dug deep into the cleared ground, creating a deep hole, until their tools hit solid rock. The metal implements rang against the granite bedrock, and the young tree felt the vibrations through his roots. The humans slowly built walls of stone in the hole, and laid down a floor of liquid ground rock, connecting the foundation to the rock ledge.

Wagons rolled up the dirt road, pulled by large horses, who snorted and heaved for breath after hauling the loads up the hills to the spot of land he called home. They brought machinery to cut trees into lumber, and other parts for this construct made of the wood. The young Norway Spruce thought certainly he might be felled to clear room. The saw chugged, slicing felled trees into boards of lumber, and as the days passed, a fresh wooden frame reached into the skies, taller than himself. A red brick column towered above the roofing frame, and though nervous, the young spruce grew fascinated with the activity, which surpassed the likes of any beaver known to his kind.

"Sorrow, sorrow for our older brethren, but fear not. They avoid you." The gentle whispering drifted to him. He shuddered in the light breezes of summer, not mollified by the soft songs of his sire, a towering Norway Spruce further up the hill. The young Spruce understood that animal life used trees for their benefits, and humans, like beavers on a grand scale, felled and used trees to construct their lodges, doing so for centuries upon centuries. They used smaller logs to burn for warmth in the cold of winter, and to cook their food. These things he knew, listening as always, to the rumblings and deep communications of the older trees around him. Their knowledge became his, through the deep tangled network of roots underground, and with the airborne communication within with every tree's respiration.

The human animals scurried around, but never threatened him, nor the twenty-five season old Big Apple adjacent to him in the field, nor the young Maple who grew near the road. The house rose from the stone foundation as the workers thrust up wooden walls and covered the roof in cedar sheets. The scent wafted on the winds, swirling around the Young Spruce. The workmen covered the cedar with strange dark grey shingling.

Soon, a small shed joined the house, sitting in north corner of the property. The family moved in just before full summer, and tilled the earth of the cleared field and planted a garden with food plants. Life quieted down and the birds returned to shelter in his boughs, and other wildlife returned to prowl the lands.

Before winter sent the first snows, the family settled in, harvesting their bounty to store in the cellar. The Norway Spruce learned the nature of the little shed, and he sent questing roots in that direction.

"Mmmmm," he murmured into the root network at his Apple and Maple companions. "Animal dung provide nutrients." Treeish mirth rippled through the ground. Smoke puffed from the brick tower. Racial memories stirred his phloem, and deep instinctual fear of fire flashed through him. His terror of the smoke diminished over time when no flame threatened him.

To the south of the house, the humans dug another hole, lined it with stones, happy when it filled with water. They covered it with a little roof, and hung a bucket from the roof with a long rope. The Young Spruce wondered at this strange contraption, until he saw a female human let the bucket drop into the hole, then turn a handle to raise it up again. The woman carried the bucket full of water into the house. Then he understood. Every living thing needed water.

The young Norway Spruce delighted in the winter winds and deep snows, enjoying the nourishment the snows brought. Each snowflake trapped nutritious nitrogen with its formation, and when melted, it released the food element into the soil. He and all his needle-leafed compatriots disliked snow-less winters. Around him, his deciduous friends slumbered.

One day after the first snows covered the lands in white, the humans dug up one of his younger siblings which grew on the property.

"Noooo!" the sapling tree protested from his stomata as the humans cut him off from the root network, and carried the little conifer into the house. They did not cut him up for firewood.

"Whyy?"The young Norway Spruce asked, fear shivering his roots and needles.

"Look, my Young Son. Brother be Christmas Tree." His sire rumbled an answer, sending a vision of the young spruce's purpose.

"Chris–stmas Tree?" He saw his sibling standing inside the house, by a window, decorated with shining objects. For a half moon, the sapling served as a Christmas tree. After the humans finished with him, they brought the young tree back out onto the land, and replanted him.

"Exciting! See and sense inside human lodge! Learn much." He babbled in a weird combination of treespeak, and human speech that the Young Spruce found difficult to understand. The youngster suffered, as he struggled to regrow roots into the frozen ground, but regretted nothing the humans did to him.

"Hurt?" the Young Spruce asked.

"Yes, hard. Cold ground stop roots. Wish to be inside."

"Why?" the Young Spruce asked his sibling, after watching the sapling struggle to reestablish proper connections with the soil. "Grow you cannot inside."

"Like being Christmas Tree! Humans sing, love. Hard explain."

"Not like it at all," The Young Spruce responded to his sibling. "Hot inside. No open sky, no sun."

"No." The sapling agreed, blowing through his stomata. "Different."

The Young Spruce sighed in the wind in a sharp song of youth and confusion, not understanding why his injured sibling wanted his way to the sun and sky blocked by human constructs. With the coming of spring, the sapling succeeded in connecting to the root network and sprouted new growth.

The family in the house roused from its semi-hibernation, sowing seeds in freshly tilled earth, and tending Big Apple and a few apple tree saplings they left in the yard. The offspring of Big Apple grew quickly under the attention, drinking in the sun, hooking their roots into the tangle underground.

****

TWO

Time passed with each cycle of seasons. The humans never used him as a Christmas tree, since his considerable height for his age prevented them from choosing him, however, many of his younger siblings served that purpose. Some survived, but many never broke bud again in spring, dying a mere moon after serving as a Christmas tree, but none of them regretted the experience. The Young Spruce shuddered in place, never wanting to find out what intrigued them so much. He slowly matured, noting each change that came to his spot on this world, growing swiftly. Birds took refuge in his sheltering boughs, and their droppings enriched the soil below.

When he reached his twenty-fourth season, new owners took over the house. The couple settled in, and raised children, and the Young Spruce enjoyed the admiration of the family as he stretched his limbs to the skies. To his delight, this couple obtained their Christmas trees from elsewhere, leaving the remnant of his siblings scattered in the area alone. The young Apple trees grew quickly, and Big Apple matured into a fine specimen at his half century mark. The Norway Spruce felt Big Apple's roots reaching across the yard to touch his own. The young house itself, connected to the bedrock, began to radiate its own displeasure or delight in inarticulate release of energies gleaned from the earth itself, which reverberated through the root network.

"House alive?" his younger sibling asked on cool day in leaf fall.

"Not as we are," their sire answered. "But like the home I shelter, stone connects to the earth. They live in their own way."

"All houses alive like this?" The Norway Spruce asked.

"Some more, some less." the old Spruce rumbled his answer. "Yours touches bedrock. I hear its songs way up here at the hilltop."

"Yes, "Big Apple agreed. "This one sings, groans and sighs. Not alive, yet is."

The Norway Spruce sighed in the breeze, and rumbled into the network, feeling pride in the special home that sat on his land.

"Yours second house on our lands. Mine first. Both special" the Young Spruce's sire chuckled with treeish laughter and pride. "We shade and protect."

"Protect humans?" The Norway Spruce asked, a bit incredulous. "They fell our brethren to build such."

"Yes, but they need us, too." his sire responded with a rumble of amusement. "House happy in shade? No?"

"Yes," the young Norway Spruce answered. "It sings when I shade."

"Good. House made from trees, so in sense are brethren. Happy house has happy humans who leave us to our task. Some humans admire us. Not all bad."

"I believe when see for self," the Norway Spruce retorted. "But will shade, protect house. Like singing house."

The young Norway Spruce grew, increasing his shade and wind-breaking abilities. The current human owners indeed admired him, but fear niggled within him always. If need arose for fuel, they might fell him with nary a regret.

During the summer of his forty-fifth season, humans planted bare wooden poles along the dirt road, stringing then with strange vines that hummed with energy, and connected the houses in a network of their own. On many of the poles, on metal branches, flameless lights hung, coming to life when the sun set each night. The Norway Spruce realized those odd things replaced the need for wood to heat and light the homes. The owners tore down the little building in the corner of the yard and constructed a new addition onto the house, which ran along the south corner. The aging home protested at first, its fear radiating from it in waves of energy, but as the workers stopped digging, and began to add new stones to create additional walls, that fused well with the old stone foundation, the old house settled down with a mumble.

The workers erected wooden walls, then concrete walls around the basement exit and the old backporch. They laid down the new metal roof on the extension, and shingled this with grey material. Workers dug the ground, lining the holes with odd stone blocks, running piping from the home to the hole. They also dug the ground between the house and the well, laying down pipe. They removed little roof and bucket and placed a removable cover on top of the well. Big trucks and horse-drawn wagons rumbled up the dirt roads bringing supplies. The Norway Spruce's fears diminished as the trucks and workers left him alone. The horses often stood in his shade, drinking water and eating grain, and he welcomed their piles of dung.

Once work ceased, he sighed, realizing no more animal dung fell to the ground from the torn down shed. His roots reached for the new construct, because though the nutrient rich dung dumped from the new addition into the underground hole, it eventually leaked into the surrounding soil. Delighted, he reached eagerly for the leaching fields, using the animal waste to power his growth.

"I reach first," Big Apple rumbled in jubilance.

"You closer," the young Spruce retorted. "But I grow fast!"

Both trees vibrated their laughter through the network.

Early leaf fall of his forty-eighth season brought torrential rains ahead of an oncoming storm. Rising winds screamed across the Lands. The Norway Spruce bowed before the gale, feeling some boughs rip free, but endured the tropical cyclone, sucking up the glut of water even as the winds tore limbs and needles from him. The storm felled his old sire, who gave way in the ferocious winds. The big spruce dropped to the ground with a tremendous thud that shook the entire area. The Young Spruce keened to the winds, as did many of the other trees. The Old One's demise left a vast empty spot in the skies on the hillside. The old house it once shaded moaned in response to the loss, and it reverberated down the hill, causing the Norway Spruce's home to sigh.

"Sad, sad, farewell old Friend!" Big Apple groaned in the savage winds. The storm mangled him, littering the lawn with his branches laden with fruit. Flooding radically altered the surrounding lands when the river over the hill flooded, and nearly wiped out the human city that straddled the river southwest of his home. The human's strange network of black vines suffered damage, many of them ripping free of their poles. The home he protected protested its loss of energy with a moan.

Once the storm spun out to sea, the Norway Spruce stood strong, drinking in the sun and carbon dioxide, using these elements to put out new growth and expel oxygen, as he raced for the open skies, happy the home he sheltered also stood firm. Humans worked from trucks to reattach the black energy vines, and soon the house hummed its contentment. The owner merely pruned Big Apple, and soon, the tree filled in the gaping holes in his canopy. He moaned his pain into the network.

"You hurt." The Young Spruce responded.

"Yes, but I heal. Soon all will be well," Big Apple assured him, but the Norway Spruce sensed the damage ran deeper than.

A few seasons passed, and the Norway Spruce sensed a big change to the roadways around him the summer he turned fifty years of age. Humans and loud machines worked, laying black odorous asphalt over the dusty dirt roads. More homes joined his on the lands. Horses became scarce, as automobiles took their places. Old Gent enjoyed the small increase in carbon dioxide in the atmosphere, taking it in to fuel more growth.

The tall Norway Spruce took the rest of the changes with nary a thought, amused at the busy beaverlike activity of the humans, including those living in the house he sheltered. The owners aged. The children moved out, but always visited their parents, bringing with them their own offspring. Many days the yard filled with human laughter and talk. The old house hummed its contentment, but the Norway Spruce felt nothing but wary tolerance. He protected and shaded the aging house, but cared little for what the humans occupying his old home said or did, as long as they left him alone.

The house took on a subtle personality of its own, its stone foundation drawing energy from the ground, It grew more feisty and expressive with collected energies each passing season. When content, it hummed and thrummed in an ancient song of stone and rock, drawing strength from its connection to the black vine network. The Young Norway Spruce felt the music thread along his roots, and thought of his sire, who loved such things.

"Ah, Young One," Big Apple rumbled, "Tis a grand song our home sings. Your sire understood these things so well, as do I."

"He did, as do I," a new voice reached him through the winds from a young Norway Spruce far up the hill. "I grow. Take his task."

"Young Brother!" The Norway Spruce cried happily from his stomata. "Happy for you."

Treeish joy vibrated the air and ground.

****

THREE

During the Norway Spruce's sixth decade, more houses sprouted along the street and beyond. The increase in human population and automobiles brought an added benefit-extra carbon dioxide. He used it to fuel his reach into the sky, growing swiftly each year, reclaiming the height he lost so long ago.

Hurricanes battered his lands in three of those ten seasons, once again tearing up the landscape with flooding and savage winds, but he lost only a few boughs. During the latest storm attack of that decade, the cyclonic winds tore his sibling's limbs, but the younger Spruce stubbornly battled the storm's fury, refusing to be downed despite his weaker root system.

"Stand tall!" The voice erupted from a young Oak sapling in the empty lot on the north side of his yard. The youngster bowed in the fierce winds, but the Norway Spruce sensed a young tree of indomitable spirit.

"We shall," The aging Norway Spruce rumbled encouragement.

The fierce storm once again ripped black vines free of the poles, causing all homes to go dark at night.

The Norway Spruce recovered swiftly once the hurricanes passed out to sea. The young Oak sprang back, vigorous and happy. Humans and their trucks returned and reattached the black vines. The homes suffered little or minor damages, but his house cried its fear of the wind to the skies days after the storm passed. He rumbled reassurances, and slowly the house ceased its fearful groaning, and once again sang its stonesong to the network.

The next spring, the family planted a large garden, and a young Plum tree in the upper section of the garden.

"Greetings. . . ." The Plum said, then chattered to the winds, and the Spruce knew the sapling originated from a nursery, raised by humans.

"Know human speech well?" The Norway Spruce asked.

"Yes," The Plum answered, and his stomata rasped with unintelligible wording. But he stopped using human speech with each passing season. The Plum grew swiftly and joined the network, learning proper treespeak.

The following season brought noisy machinery to the Norway Spruce's lands. Trucks carrying loads of the liquid grey ground up stone called concrete rolled onto the property. The owner built a strange lodge of the poured concrete, working furiously to complete the odd building that sat partially underground to the south of the well. The heavy machinery roared, vibrating the ground, but stayed well away from the trees as they dug the earth.

"What kind of lodge that be?" the Young Norway asked.

"Not know," Big Apple answered.

"Owner call it "bomb shelter," the Maple up by the road replied. "I know not what that means, but our owner stores food and other things inside."

The Norway Spruce and his friends wondered for a while, but soon, the odd construct sat unused, becoming part of the land and they ignored it. The Christmas seasons during that time, brought a new tradition to the Lands, in which humans decorated young conifers in the yard, as well as houses, with strings of bright colorful lights. The Norway Spruce sighed in the snowy breezes. His younger sibling, chattered excitedly, his ragged branches swaying in the winds.

"Pretty lights on me?" he asked.

"No," the Norway Spruce answered. "Too big now."

"Oh." his sibling sighed with disappointment.

A few seasons later, on a warm summer day, the homeowner's spouse died. Sadness permeated the home and property, worsening when the owner passed away several years later, lounging on the home's front porch. Even the old house released its grief in unintelligible creaks and groans. The Norway Spruce felt some apprehension, since these humans lived in his house for forty-two of his sixty-six seasons. The couple's children sold the home to another family, and he sensed their admiration of him. They understood his task to shade and shelter the house well enough, but he felt no connection to them.

As his seventh decade passed into his eighth, he towered into the sky, well over one-hundred-and-twenty feet tall, sensing changes far and wide across his lands. The lake down the hill reflected sunlight to his upper boughs. He saw far up the hill where his much younger sibling shaded the home his sire once did, young, strong and tall. Along the street, new homes sprouted, including one in the lot where the young Oak stood, taller and thicker in response to the storms seasons ago.

"Have own house to protect now," the Oak rumbled happily into the network.

"You grow strong," The Old Norway Spruce replied.

"You strong! I be like you one day," the Oak responded. The Norway Spruce's branches grew until he almost touched the house itself. His shade protected his house from summer's heat, and his thick branches shielded the home from winter's fierce winds. He sensed easily the temperament of the old house. It groaned in the heat, sang as his shade passed over it, and creaked in the cold. He sang his conifer songs in the wind, joining the old house in symphony.Birds sang along in harmony.

One summer, workers arrived, and tore the old home's grey clapboards off, causing the feisty house to grumble to its foundation. The construction workers replaced them with shingles the owner then painted a pale yellow.

"Old lodge look like sun." the old Norway Spruce rumbled with mirth. The house responded with a wave of energy that swirled out from under the new material. The trees rumbled mirth into the network. The Old Norway Spruce liked the color better than the drab grey. It reflected more sunlight to his questing boughs.

The next few seasons brought more homes to the neighborhood, and noisy machinery that dug up the roadsides, laying pipes and drains. The Norway Spruce did not understand the purpose until the owners covered up the old well. Somehow, humans managed to bring water inside the houses with the underground pipes.

One warm summer day, early in his eighth decade of life, much to his dismay, the homeowner and a few helpers, surrounded the Big Apple, examining him.

"They come to fell me," Big Apple muttered into the network, resigned to the inevitable.

"No!" The Norway Spruce protested.

"The deep rot eats me from within. You were right. Storm damage so many seasons ago tore me bad enough so water seeps into my heartwood and caused this decay," Big Apple murmured. "Do not grieve my friend. I have lived long. Over a century on the Lands. It is my time."

The humans started up their chainsaw, and felled the Big Apple with the roaring death machine. Leaving Big Apple's stump, they cleared away the grand tree's body, sending it through something that chopped the wood into bits. His offspring all keened their grief.

Before the Norway Spruce grieved for his old friend, the owner approached him, purpose in his stride, the threatening noisy machine in hand. The Norway Spruce shuddered in alarm. His whole being screamed NOOOO into the network and atmosphere. Why him? No rot ate at his heartwood yet! Ice never ripped him apart! He towered strong and powerful!

Up a long ladder the man climbed, and suddenly, the machine roared to life. The startled Norway Spruce felt it saw into his upper branches. The limbs dropped to the yard below with thuds that shook the ground. His fellow yardmates, all now mature, keened in shock. The Red Maples on the northern and the western property lines, the Sugar Maple up near the road, and the apple trees down the lawn, thundered the alarm to the underground network.

The younger trees, including the stout Oak in the next yard, the young Plum Tree, a set of sapling White birches across the street, the two very young Sugar Maples dominating the yard across the street, added higher vibrations of fear to the old network. The ground rumbled with astonishment as trees up and down the neighborhood reacted to the attacks.

Even the old house groaned to its foundation, unhappy with the attack on its protector. After what seemed an eternity, the men climbed down his trunk, and chipped up his felled boughs, then put the chainsaw away.

The Norway Spruce stood, shocked and upset at the topping of his upper boughs and the felling of his yardmate. He missed Big Apple, but hated more that he no longer saw for miles, nor sensed as keenly, and the refracted light off the lake barely touched him now. His roots reached deep and far, so he sprouted new growth, vowing to replace the amputated limbs as fast as possible.

On winter days, when the snows bent his boughs over, he yearned to once again touch the old house, whose foundation entangled with the underground network of tree roots. Why must humans be so insensitive?

He shuddered in the gentle breezes, trying to take comfort in the fact he still stood, and not lying on the ground as chipper fodder. He did not even mind that the owner hung a swing from his lower limb years ago, but why did he have to lop off his glorious top that reached for the sun?

"Careless giant beavers," he rumbled to his yardmates.

"Sad, sad," the Plum muttered.

"Not right, not right," the Oak moaned.

Oh, no Brother," his young sibling up the hill cried. "Not right at all!"

The Norway Spruce rumbled his displeasure into the root network. Why his sire ever thought humans who respected and revered his kind existed baffled him. His age and wisdom accrued over his eight decades of life told him otherwise.

* *

FOUR

Time passed, and the Old Norway Spruce grew, determined to regain his former glory. Late in his eighth decade, the family living in the old house split off part of the property. One morning, massive machines thundered onto the Lands and destroyed the odd bomb shelter lodge, clearing it from the land.

The Norway Spruce shivered in terror, but the massive vehicles stayed well away from him, and his fear diminished. Another piece of equipment roared onto the land, digging deep into the ground. Then, the big concrete trucks arrived and a new house's concrete foundation rose from the hole. As the season progressed, the house grew steadily, until the workers finally completed the dwelling.

The owner then moved into new construct, leaving the older home empty. Old Maple up near the road rustled his leaves in delight.

"I have house to shade now! Still shade yours, but have mine, too."

"I shade too!" The Norway Spruce's tattered sibling added. "This house now mine, too."

"We shade and protect together," the Old Maple rumbled in delight.

The Norway Spruce's old house responded with groans, unhappy, but the new house, still fresh and disconnected from the Lands, never reacted to the old house. The home grumbled and groaned, until another family moved into it when the Old Norway Spruce turned seventy-seven years old.

To the north of the house, the new owners built a new parking area, which formed a steep bank behind itself.

Motorcycles roared to and from the house after one of the occupants built a little bike shed below the back porch. They also covered the yellow shingles with light metal clapboard, which shone green, and rattled alarms in strong winds. The Old Norway Spruce did not mind, since the humans left him alone. The old house settled down, content again, not releasing angry energies from its stone foundation, enjoying the happiness that radiated from the children. Soon, it sang its stonesong back to the network.

To the Norway Spruce's dismay, a season later, a wicked ice storm roared in early that winter, coating everyone in thick ice. Strong winds buffeted everyone, and ice crackled as it thickened on everything.

"Owww" A moan caught his attention and to his shock, his younger sibling, who never fully recovered from his stint as a Christmas tree, broke under the merciless ice. Large limbs cracked, then tore free of the smaller tree's trunk, revealing the heartwood, ripping phloem away in chunks.

"Ow," the younger spruce groaned. "Dying."

"No! Fight! Grow!" The Norway Spruce demanded of his sibling.

"No! Grow!" the Oak added.

"Nooo!" the Old Maple cried.

"Grow! Grow!" the sibling up the hill shouted from his stomata.

"Try," the younger spruce mumbled into the root network, but as the winter progressed, the sibling weakened, and lost his battle. His needles browned, and by spring, he stood, battered, broken, and unresponsive. The owner of the new home took a dreaded chain saw, and cut down the dead sibling. The Old Norway Spruce sang a dirge to the winds. The old house thrummed a woeful melody to the bedrock, and the trees on the Lands joined them in the sad treeish tribute.

During the next few seasons, the Old Spruce welcomed new young trees to the area, including a young Blue Spruce across the street that wore Christmas lights each season. He felt melancholy emotion, remembering how much his younger sibling loved the new light tradition during the human's Christmas season. He also lost friends as the little cluster of Big Apple's offspring fell prey to the dreaded chainsaw as the owner expanded the garden.

The Norway Spruce cared not for any of the humans that sat in his shade or played on the lawns. He thought his sire wrong in believing any humans that appreciated his kind existed. He never forgot the loss of his top boughs, and enjoyed the snows of winter that kept humans inside and nourished his massive root system.

Over the next few seasons, the owners' children grew up and moved away. During his tenth decade, the aging couple contemplated leaving, and he almost felt sorry for the woman, whose sadness permeated yard. The old house groaned its unease in the winds. The Old Norway Spruce turned his attention inward, caring only about regaining what he lost, and concentrated every season to catch the sun and grow.

****

FIVE

On a clear spring afternoon, in his ninety-first year, he noted a young human couple walking around the house, and knew prospective new owners considered the house he sheltered. Despite the fine weather, where the sun shone from a deep blue sky, and fluffy white clouds rode the breezes, a stab of alarm stirred his phloem, As much as he ignored the current owners, he knew they loved his land. The old house, quiet for many mooncycles, radiated with excited energy the Old Norway Spruce did not comprehend.

The two humans strode down into the yard, and the young woman looked up at him. As her eyes swept over him, he felt something, an odd feeling he never before experienced with any of the previous owners, not even the humans that owned the house for so long, many decades ago.

He never paid attention to the humans' language before, but suddenly, the human's yammering made sense to him. He suddenly felt no fear, and excitement from the feisty old house infected him. The Plum tree suddenly chattered like in the days of his sapling youth.

"This one is different" his airborne song said, and his roots shook into the network a sudden joy.

"Different!" A few remaining offspring of Big Apple on the adjoining property agreed.

"What a beautiful Old Gent," the woman said, looking up, emotion radiating from her so strong it permeated his entire aura. When she directed her talk directly at him, the Old Spruce sang his conifer song to the winds.

"You remind me of the New Hampshire forests, and the grand old trees near my grandmom's house. I love the sound of the wind in your boughs." She turned to her mate. "I like this place!"

The young man glanced up at Old Gent, and nodded his agreement. The couple walked back around the house, and when they drove off, the Old Gent of a Norway Spruce felt strange emotions, and wished the female human would return. He knew the house changed owners once again, but he felt sudden alarm. What if that couple failed in their bid to buy the home? Who might return to occupy the old homestead?

For the first time in his long life, he cared who lived in the old home, and so did the house, whose inarticulate anxiety rolled out from the foundation in waves. The summer dragged by, and the old couple did not leave. Perhaps the old home did not sell after all. Old Gent sighed in the wind, enduring the longest summer season of his life.

Leaf fall arrived, and as his deciduous yardmates dropped their leaves and sank into slumber. Old Gent decided nothing would change, until, on a cool autumn day, the old couple surprised him, and moved out. The house stood empty, yet eager and hopeful. Old Gent waited for only the fifth owner in nine decades to occupy his old house.

One cool evening, a pickup truck pulled into the parking area, and human activity filled the house. Busy like the beavers they reminded him of, the young humans scurried in and out of the house, which radiated joy into the network. Old Gent stirred, recognizing a voice, and yes, the female human he connected with mooncycles ago carried items into the house. Warm light spilled out into the yard, and the old house thrummed so forcefully it vibrated its own foundation.

The next day, the couple worked, hauling stuff in the pickup truck from their old residence, and in one of the last hauls, three very young naked Tuliptree saplings stood in the truck, yammering in treespeak with human words. The Plum Tree rumbled with delight, stirring to awareness, and his deeper tones joined the baby trees' excited voices. Old Gent grumbled deep in his roots.

"Should they not be slumbering in dormancy?"

"Dug up! Exciting!" A tiny Mugo Pine and a sprig of an Arborvitae, sitting behind the saplings, joined the noise. Old Gent rumbled reassurances to the babies.

During the next few days, the female human worked planting the baby trees, her hands gentle, and she spoke to them. They spoke back, but Old Gent knew she did not hear them. She planted the oldest sapling beside the driveway on the north side, yards away from Old Gent's long time yardmate, a stout Red Maple. The brazen little Tuliptree threaded a few new cells of growth into the ground and connected to the network. Her attempts to communicate amused Old Gent and he reached for her. Her two sister trees took cue, and copied her.

Later that Fall, before the ground froze solid, seedlings joined the tree community; two tiny Dwarf Apples, a Chokecherry, a Silver Maple, a Redbud, a Mountain Ash, a Black Walnut, and a Blue Spruce. All chattered in that weird combination of slow treespeak and fast human speech.

That Christmas season, Old Gent watched as the young Spruce across the street donned his Christmas lights again. Suddenly, he thought it quite beautiful and fetching, as the home's new owner's love of the season drew him in. He comprehended nothing of the concepts in her mind of why humans in general celebrated Christmas, but he understood her reasons.

Her reverence and love of his kind reverberated through him, and he accepted that stringing lights on conifers showed appreciation and respect for his needled brethren. For his home's new owner, Christmas trees ruled the season, and that pleased him immensely. His view of humans changed, and though he still saw them as giant naked beavers, his distrust of them diminished. Perhaps, this one, indeed, might be the type of human his sire spoke of so many seasons ago.

The winter progressed after the Christmas season, blanketing the land in deep nourishing snows. It took many moons, during the cold of winter and early spring, for the newcomers' roots to reach deeper into the ground. Old Gent's roots easily reached under the driveway and the entire yard, to touch the baby trees. He waited for spring, intrigued by all the young seedlings and saplings new to his Lands.

****

SIX

Spring arrived in Old Gent's ninety-second season, and the baby Tuliptree by the parking area broke bud one warm breezy morning. Sunlight bathed her three foot tall body. As Old Gent touched roots with all the waking youngsters, awareness flooded him with knowledge he never imagined. The Plum Tree's excited communications suddenly made sense to him. Up the lawn into the other yard, the old Maple responded, rumbling the ground. Across the street the twin Sugar Maples reacted, along with their older Red Maple brethren down the lawn from the baby Tuliptree, and the network connected with comprehension.

In mere moments, a shocking, short time for Old Gent, he and his landmates understood the cries of the little sapling. A high excited vibration of a voice erupted from the stomata of her tiny but fast-growing leaves, and she spoke with human words and treespeak again.

"I Sunrise!" the little Tuliptree announced. "Wake! Wake! Spring here!"

"Yesss," Old Gent rumbled with joy. "Little One, spring is here."

"I Sunrise! You?"

"Human call me Old Gent. I Old Gent. Welcome all new saplings."

"Human my Momma! She raise me. Take me with her when she move away. Happy happy place this is! She now your Momma, too."

"Yes, perhaps, though I old enough to be her grandsire," Old Gent agreed with a treeish chuckle, and sang his conifer song in the spring winds. All the older trees rumbled their delight. Birds sang out their mating calls, using his great height to perch and claim territory.

"Lucky be you," the Oak said. "To have such human on your land. We all sense the love she gives."

"Yes," Old Gent replied. "If lucky, she stay here long long time."

The old trees rumbled agreement. All the young trees hummed and muttered to each other, joyous when their Momma, now his Momma too, tended them with loving hands. Old Gent quivered with emotion when Momma planted a rose bush in Big Apple's rotting stump. He wanted to tell her about Big Apple, but took delight in her appreciation for the old tree's stump, amused that she thought it belonged to a sibling of his.

Old Gent felt protective, not only of the happy old house now, but of its occupants. Never before had he cared for any human, but with every touch of Momma's hands on his trunk or his new spring growth, which she stroked with loving fingers, he cared more every mooncycle. He sensed her love of his kind, and new feelings coursed through his almost a century old body.

He yearned to understand her, and learned from the new saplings the complexities of human speech. He enjoyed, as never before, the activity of the humans. Happiness and security flooded his being for the first time since humans invaded his Lands, but circumstance soon threatened his newfound love. That summer, one warm sunny afternoon, he overheard the owners talking with the neighbors.

"We may have to move," Momma said, sadness in her voice. "The place we work at was just sold and is moving away. We just got this place, and I love it. I don't want to move."

"We don't want you to move either," the owner of the other home said.

Dismay and dread flashed through Old Gent, followed by an anxiety he never before experienced. Old Gent wished in that moment he never learned human speech, and screamed denials from his stomata, shutting out the rest of the human conversation.

He trembled in the summer winds, unable to believe the horrible luck of encountering humans he cherished, only to have them move away. The old house reacted with a deep groan of denial. Old Gent fretted for many mooncycles, until Momma and her mate came to sit in his shade after working in the yard one warm late summer day. She sat on the old wooden swing, and her mate set out a lounge.

"Well, I am glad we are here to stay." she said, looking up into Old Gent's boughs. "Tennessee was way too hot anyway."

"We will be fine," he responded. "At least they won't be closing for a while. Gives us both a chance to look for new work."

Old Gent's phloem hummed with sudden joy. True to their word, they did not sell the old house and stayed put. Momma's spouse found a new job, as did Momma, but soon after, Momma stopped going off to work every morning. She hobbled on painful feet, and even after they healed, stayed home, which pleased Old Gent.

Life settled down, and many days, his owners' entire family visited, and lounged in his shade. Momma's little nephew swung on Old Gent's swing on those fun-filled days, when Momma laughed with siblings, in-laws, and other family. Old Gent serenaded them all with his songs. The old house hummed, drawing extra energy from the loving family. When Momma herself sat on the swing, enjoying Old Gent's presence in quieter moments, he felt ecstasy. She always spoke to him, infusing him with joy and love.

Her mate, whom Momma called Poppa, when referencing their feline housemates, also admired him. Old Gent decided Momma's spouse fit as his Poppa. More than mere caretakers of Old Gent's house and lands, these humans opened his heartwood to a deep love he never before experienced, and now he understood why all the young trees looked to the home's owners as their momma and poppa. He wished his sire lived to know his wisdom rang true down the decades. Such humans did indeed exist!

****

SEVEN

A few seasons passed, and the Tuliptree youngsters all stood three times their original height, growing incredibly fast, developing into strong saplings which spread their big leaves to the sun. The Plum, at a half century of age, flowered profusely each spring, covering himself in stunning white blossoms. The baby Dwarf Apples grew in his shadow, babbling and yearning to reach his height. The sapling Silver Maple, Mountain Ash, Black Walnut, and Chokecherry stretched boughs to the skies, trying to match their swift growing Tuliptree sisters, but remained slow growing compared to Old Gent and the Tuliptrees.

The little Redbud disappeared that first winter, eaten by a deer. Arborvitae, planted a mere foot out from the foundation of the front porch of the old house, and Mugo, set in the corner by the bathroom, grew very slow. Old Gent learned Poppa grafted the little Pine and propagated Arborvitae for a college class years before. Momma nurtured the Mugo in the years prior to this move.

The young Colorado Blue Spruce, whom Momma called Blue Dude, grew only a bit faster than those two. Blue Dude stood barely to Momma's knees after those three seasons.

"Slowpokes," Sunrise teased her yardmates.

"Dangerous to grow so fast," Blue Dude retorted.

"Not dangerous." Sunrise replied. "Catch the sun! Grow fast!"

"Want to grow fast!" Arborvitae lamented.

"I supposed to stay small!" Mugo protested.

"All grow different," Old Gent admonished the youngsters.

"Sorry," Sunrise whistled through her large stomata. "Not mean hurt."

"Know," Blue Dude replied.

Old Gent rumbled with approval. He never liked interspecies bickering, nor did his sire. He planned to teach the youngsters here that wisdom.

During his ninety-fourth season, one summer morning broke hot and humid. Weak sunlight shone through thickening clouds touched with a greenish hue. As the morning turned to afternoon, the oppressive humidly increased. The clouds darkened to the northwest, their green taint deepening to a muddy hue. Old Gent felt a warning vibration in the ground, which washed through the soil like ripples in a pond. The hot air cloaked him like a thick blanket, and not a breath of wind touched his boughs. All the ground dwelling wildlife in the area took refuge or left the area.

The alarm increased, undulating through the ground in waves of pain and terror. He scanned his territory, questing for more knowledge, sensing the dread originated from very ancient trees some distance away. Their fear and agony shivered through his heartwood, and all the trees felt the distant terror. Above, the sun shone through very thick humid air, a pale circle of dim light, and slowly, the oncoming clouds covered the sun. The birds silenced, and many took flight, leaving the area in haste.

"Bad weather come," the Oak mumbled, echoed by all the Maples, and aging Apple trees. "Very bad."

"Dangerous," he heard his sibling up the hill add.

"Scared," Sunrise cried, in a high voice reminiscent of her baby days. She stood a mere twelve feet tall. Old Gent rumbled inarticulately, trying to soothe her, but he barely contained his own rising fears when he sensed the oncoming storm. To the northwest, the skies blackened to night sky dark, and lightning flashed. Thunder followed, shaking everyone to their roots.

Winds suddenly lashed the landscape, as the squall line rushed towards them. Old Gent heard his Momma calling for her and Poppa's cat, who hid under the neighbor's storage shed, heard the terror in her voice, and sensed dread radiate from the old house. Though frightened by the oncoming storm, Old Gent felt protectiveness rise up his phloem to infuse every needle on his 110 foot body. The wind rose to cyclone force, driving the rain ahead of it, spinning the torrential downpour in every direction.

Old Gent remembered the hurricanes of his youth, but unlike those storms, the winds this day whirled in all directions, so he stood firm, waiting for his enemy, a twister bearing down on the old house and owners he loved. The furious winds spun around him, and he swung his limbs in the tornado's attack. He heard the high screams of his fellow trees above the roar of the storm, and, struggled to stand tall and strong, as the squall line and its twisters reached the property he protected. The tornado mowed the ground clean on the property line, then lifted from the ground, driven by eddies and air currents created by Old Gent's massive form. The Plum tree blew over with a high scream, unable to withstand the winds. The younger Maples bowed so far over in the gale, their crowns almost touched the ground. The Oak bent away from the cyclonic fury.

The cyclone shredded leaves and needles, plastering them to every side of the old house, which roared its own terror and outrage to the storm. Old Gent knew it tried to protect the owners it loved as much as he, urging him to fight with every atom of his tall strong body.

The young Tuliptrees shrieked as the mindless tornado flattened them to the ground. The twister spun Old Gent's upper body until it split asunder, stressing the lower half of his century old trunk with such torque, he cracked almost to his very roots. The swing attached to a lower bough caught the chaotic winds, tearing the limb free of his body.

He groaned into the underground network, hearing so many trees answering in kind. Forty eight feet of his glorious height, which he spent over two decades to regrow, snapped free, spinning in the wild winds, and dropped to the yard, just missing Poppa's gas grill. He screamed defiance from his stomata as the twister hopped over both homes, to touch ground across the street, decimating a stand of lovely young White Pines.

It raced up the hill, battled and uprooted his young brother, whose screams of protest echoed down the hill. The twister then left the area, leaving Old Gent, his brethren, and his beloved land shattered and torn. The old house, however, stood firm, leaves plastered on its surface, gutters and strips of siding dangling like remnant autum leaves. Old Gent stood, relieved the old house sat safe, even as his battered body screamed agony.

His homeowners rushed out of the house, shocked and upset. Momma raced around, crying, as she and Poppa used rope and tent stakes to right her sapling Tuliptrees that lay in different directions in the yard, a testament to the twister's mindless wrath. Momma and Poppa stood Sunrise back up, and tethered her firmly. She wailed into the network, with her sisters. Poppa found some type of mechanism that lifted the Old Plum, pulling him straight again. Both lamented the loss of Old Gent's top.

"I grow strong now. Never fall again," Sunrise wailed. Old trees moaned. Younger trees screamed. The Old Maple by the road stood, mangled and broken, half of his body scattered on the lawn and road beyond. Old Gent saw his old friend's heartwood filled with rot, caused by damages wrought from the hurricanes that rolled through here in their youth. He felt the crack that curved down both sides of his trunk, and resins oozed from the wound in response.

In the days following the attack, the roar of chainsaws filled the air as humans cleaned up the broken bodies of trees. A man came to him with a saw, and Old Gent felt grief and disbelief that his beloved Momma allowed someone to fell him.

To his relief, the man only cleaned up the torn, twisted shattered stubs, pruned the rest, then left him alone. Old Gent gathered his strength and strove to replace what the twister took from him. He needed to grow and protect the house from the blazing sun and winter winds. He ignored the water and ice that thwarted his efforts to heal his enormous trunk. He healed the northside crack, leaving behind a scar, but the southside wound turned into a crevice. Though he filled the wound with resins, water seeped into the crack, and with each freeze and thaw cycle, he sensed the slow decay of his heartwood.

Despite the slow cancer of internal rot, Old Gent's phloem remained strong and healthy, and he grew taller each year. He yearned to reach the 100 foot mark once again.

❋❋❋

EIGHT

Life settled down and time passed. Wildlife once again passed through the Lands, and birds nested in his boughs.The humans he loved hosted many picnics and family gatherings under the shade of his great boughs. They added flower gardens and revived the fallow garden down the lawn. The neighbors added a young Hybrid Poplar in their front yard, and the skinny little sapling greeted everyone with excitement that spring after the horrendous storm.

"Greetings! Grow fast, so fast!"

"No fast like me!" Sunrise responded.

"Faster!" the Poplar chortled, and their race for the skies began. The young Poplar stretched branches to the skies at more than a meter a season.

"Poplar faster," Old Gent chuckled at Sunrise, whose three feet a season fell short of the mark.

"Know," Sunrise replied cheerfully. "But still try! Momma proud of me!"

That summer, the Poplar's people brought in big machines to the lands, which dug a hole in the yard. A big cement truck rumbled in to pour the walls in the hole, and the workers laid down a concrete deck around the hole, then they lined it with material the color of the sky. They posed no danger to the trees, and Old Gent's humans appreciated the sparkling swimming pool during the hot days of summer.

Old Gent tolerated the disturbance to his root system that summer, knowing how much his Momma loved swimming. He enjoyed the extra water he received, when the neighbor, who once lived in the home on his land, piped the excess water onto the side lawn adjacent to him. With his roots covering so much area, he easily drank up the water.

Over the seasons, many cats joined Momma's Mandee, who survived the tornado attack unscathed. He wished Momma's felines succeeded in catching squirrels. One, a black and white of a breed Momma called Maine Coon, named Demon, tried his best, but fell out of one of the Maples across the street, fatally injuring himself. He crawled to the back porch where Momma found his body. Momma's intense grief infected everyone for many seasons. Another feline, whom Momma called Phantom, worked to catch the grey bushy-tailed rodents, but despite his size, speed and strength, the big cat failed to help eradicate tree rodents. Old Gent grumbled with dismay as the squirrels used him as a giant nest. He minded not the birds, but the grey rodents created a mess and dug into his damaged heartwood. He wished they stayed aground like the rabbits and other furry inhabitants of the Lands.

During the spring of his ninety-eighth season, Momma brought home a tiny sprig of a conifer, and planted the baby near the young Silver Maple.

"Greetings little one," Old Gent murmured to the fingerling.

"Greetings!" the baby responded.

"Grow and be strong," Sunrise said to the tiny Norway Spruce. "Welcome to our lands."

"Will! Happy," the seedling trilled into the network.

One warm summer day, one of Momma's felines, a short-legged stout little stray, chased by a dog, scurried up Old Gent's trunk and huddled on a thick limb not long after the little seedling Norway Spruce put out her first questing roots. No matter how much Momma cajoled the cat, he refused to come down, and Old Gent knew the short-legged feline found it difficult to descend his great trunk with his stubby legs. He stared down at everyone, but did not make a sound. Time ticked by and the short-legged feline huddled on Old gent's limb, afraid to move.

A neighbor finally brought a ladder, climbed up and grabbed Munchkin by the nape of the neck and handed him to Momma. Old Gent rumbled with mirth. He knew that the short legged stray cat now belonged to his home and lands.

■■

NINE

Time marched into the future. Sunrise rocketed into the sky, turning a stunning gold each autumn, her trunk gaining so much girth, she looked far older than her mere couple of decades.

"Nothing knock me down again," she said each spring. Her siblings grew swiftly as well, and Sunset filled in the gaping hole left by the twister in the line of trees and bushes on the western property line. Their sibling behind the garden followed suit, but she did not grow quite as quickly as her sisters. Each spring and summer her leaves emerged smaller and smaller, and Old Gent felt a tug of concern.

The Hybrid Poplar shot into the skies, overtaking even Sunrise in the race to reach the sun, and their friendly competitive spirit amused Old Gent. Arborvitae sped up his growth, surprising everyone, taking joy that he soon shaded the front of the house. The dwarf Norway Spruce seedling Momma dubbed Little Princess grew slowly, as her kind did, but she developed a pert prim shape.

Old Gent listened to the chatter all the young trees sent into the network, and though content, felt himself weaken with each season. The hated squirrels nested in the upper part of his trunk, digging in heartwood turned mulch, hastening the decay. The felines worked to hunt them, but none caught a single squirrel.

In the howling winds of a Nor'easter or the squall of a summer thunderstorm, he feared toppling on the home he protected during his century on this land. Each

spring he put out new growth, enjoying when Momma stroked the young sprouts. She always came to him for solace when something upset her, such as the loss of one of the cats, or family problems, or any other of life's upsets that concerned humans.

He sang his songs in the breezes, dreading the day he might cause her such distress. In his hundred-and-sixth year, he stood, tall, yet ragged, but still shading the home from summer's brutal afternoon sun, and broke the force of winter's gales.

Two seasons later, in early autumn, he opened his cones, letting his seeds fly on the winds. Three caught in a weird eddy of air, settled in the gravel near the grill, while the other two nestled in a crack near the foundation. Old Gent rumbled his joy, finally succeeding to land a few where Momma might find them. His offspring dotted the Lands, but until this spring, none sprouted so close to him.

The autumn winds howled from the west on a clear day in his hundred-and-eighth season. Old Gent's trunk creaked, but he sang his conifer song in the gale, until sudden terror undulated through the underground network when the Hybrid Poplar shrilled pain to the winds. One of her three trunks went down under the strong winds, landing with a thwack across the lawns, driveway, and into the road, missing Old Gent's beloved home's front porch roof by several feet.

"Ow, ow, ow . . .," she wailed.

"Noooo! Poplar girl! Nooo!" Arborvitae shouted from his stomata in shock.

"Noooo!" Mugo cried. "Oh, no my friend!"

"Multiple trunks, bad bad thing," Old Gent rumbled.

"Why?"Arborvitae asked, anguish in his tone.

"Make weakness," Old Gent answered gently.

"Oh, no," Sunrise whispered into the network, and Old Gent knew the beautiful Tuliptree understood her friend's fate. The following day, chainsaws roared, cutting up not only the rotted downed trunk, but also felling the hapless young Poplar's remaining two trunks. Sunrise screamed her grief into the network as the killing machines destroyed her diseased friend. Old Gent rumbled condolences, but Sunrise wailed to the autumn skies. Old Gent knew the danger of multiple trunks, but no one pruned them from the poor tree in her youth. Old Gent felt this a bad omen, but let it slide to the back of his thoughts as fall turned to winter.

The deciduous trees slept as the snows fell, covering the world in gentle soothing blankets of white that protected young trees and ground from bitter winds and frigid temperatures. Sunrise slumbered, her grief abated. Old Gent rested, awaiting spring, planning to keep on growing, anticipating Momma's hands on his spring growth.

On a late winter day in his hundred-and-nineth season, a snow squall screamed across the Lands, and Old Gent groaned as the fierce winds tugged mercilessly at him. One big limb, weakened by rot, ripped free of him and dropped to the ground with a booming thud. The wind moaned and whistled through the hole on his trunk, showing him just how

far his heartwood decayed since that fateful battle with the tornado.

Momma arrived home later that morning and saw the damage. He sensed her deep fear and dread for him, and also her denial. Time slowed as her emotions reached him. As the snow melted and the days warmed, she always gazed up at him, tears in her eyes, apologizing, and Old Gent keenly felt her love and heartbreak, knowing his humans made a difficult decision. Unlike other humans in his long life, his Momma agonized over felling trees.

Weariness filled him, and he waited for the fateful day, thankful most of his yardmates still slumbered in dormancy. Though Old Gent's phloem remained healthy, giving him the power to grow, he knew his massive trunk he needed for support no longer possessed the strength to support his old and new growth. The decay reached deep down his trunk, ending a few feet above the ground. He creaked in the winds, and knew another savage wind might topple him onto the old house he loved. That thought disturbed him deeply.

One cool cloudy day snow flurried from grey skies. Not a breath of air stirred his boughs. Momma came out and plucked cones from his downed limb. She walked over and laid a hand on his trunk, and her voice quavered.

"I'm so sorry, my Old Gent. I don't want this. I will miss you more than you can ever know." She pulled her hand away and walked back to the downed limb. Old Gent wanted her to hear him, to let her know all was all right. He knew his time was near, and accepted the inevitable. He preferred to be felled, rather than fall and damage or hurt the old house and its beloved owners. She passed under a bough, and Old Gent used all of his strength to snag needles into her hair. She stopped, slapping her hand to her head, then looked up. The bough hung it its place, moving slightly.

"Did you . .?" she trailed off, and walked under the offending bough several times, standing on tiptoe, but the bough remained above her head. "You did somehow? Didn't you? How? There isn't a breath of wind!"

Old Gent rumbled, knowing she heard nothing, yet somehow, she understood. She gazed up at him, and he sensed her grief.

"I know it must be done. You may have accepted it, but I haven't," she said softly, before gathering up the cones in gentle hands and walking into the house. "You'll leave a hole in my yard and heart that will never heal!"

The first warm sunny day since the squall tore him apart, brought delight to Old Gent, when all five of his seeds sprouted into stout little seedlings. The continuation of spring days brought his humans from the house, and they worked in the yard, taking advantage of the early warmth and waxing sunshine. Old Gent waited, and watched as they spied his seedlings. Momma glanced up at him, tearful, yet smiling.

"Thank you, Old Gent, for this priceless gift! I promise to care for them for as long as I live."

The babies shrilled excitedly, and he rumbled to them, parting much wisdom along the network. Their tiny roots assimilated all he sent, before Momma dug them up and placed them in protective pots in the garden.

"Papa, we'll grow and be strong, like you." the largest seedling said in treespeak.

"You must, for ye shall take my place here." he responded, and the seedlings protested, disturbing Sunrise, whose sap began to rise a moon ago.

"Be calm my little ones. Grow strong." Old Gent soothed them.

The winds blew hard and chilly the day the tree men came for him. As they methodically clipped boughs and limbs, working their way down his great height, he groaned. Sawdust billowed on the strong breezes. His offspring cried in shrill voices from the garden, and Sunrise awoke. Her utter dismay, shock and grief stirred the rest of the trees. The old house moaned a stonesong dirge. Old Gent rumbled one last

time as they cut into his main trunk.

"Must be so. Disease makes me too weak to protect. My time is done. Do not grieve," he assured all his yardmates. As his main trunk toppled over, it hit the ground with a thump, and cracked into two hollow pieces. With a rumble, Old Gent let go of life. His life energy flowed out of his battered body, backlashing along his extensive root system, and followed the tangle of roots. His essence raced under the earth, backwashed against the old foundation of the house, then zipped up into the nearest of his offspring.

****

TEN

The jolt of energy entered the baby Norway Spruce, then rippled out to his siblings. New awareness flooded his tiny seedling body, as the tree men cleared away the last of his sire's ancient body. They left behind a vast empty wasteland where the old one once stood. He saw Momma crying. Memories not his own filled his being, and he called out to Momma.

"No cry! No cry. Young Gent and brothers here! We grow fast!"

Young Gent kept his word, and he and his tiny bothers grew quickly that season, pleasing Momma, but she still wept many days. All the trees in the yard mourned the felling of Old Gent once bud break awakened them, particularly the Tuliptree by the driveway. As she aroused fully from her winter nap, she howled her agony of loss into the network.

"Noooooo! Old Gent! Old friend, gone, gone now, too! Why, why must we all die?"

"No weep grand Sunrise! Young Gent here!" Young Gent called to her with excitement. She abruptly dropped her communication to a soft rumble.

"So you are," Sunrise rumbled, recognizing the old spirit in his young body. "Yes, you are."

"No weep."

"No, but yard sooo empty. Miss your sire." Sunrise murmured, but she no longer disturbed the trees and house with her anguish.

As spring waxed warm, Sunrise's sister unfurled tiny leaves smaller by far than the previous season. Momma noticed, studied her, and the Tuliptree shivered, mumbling her discomfort to the rootnet below ground. Young Gent wondered what might happen. A few days later, on a grey drizzly day, a tree surgeon arrived and cut away a large root curving around the base of one of Sunrise's sister's trunk. The Tuliptree endured the work, but Young Gent worried. The tree's leaves stayed small, and Young Gent knew Momma feared losing Sunrise's sister. Sunrise rumbled, entwining tiny roots across the yard, trying to reach her sister.

"No fear, Sister. I not die." Sunrise's sister assured everyone.

In early autumn, workmen drove into the yard again, and Young Gent felt a spasm of dread, until he realized they carefully brought in a large, young Norway Spruce sapling. They planted him in the ground several feet down the lawn from Old Gent's hallowed spot. Momma hovered over the newcomer like a bird caring for its young. Young Gent quivered with a mix of excitement and jealousy.

"You grow and make Momma happy," he whistled into the wind.

"I will, young one."

"I Young Gent. I son of Old Gent. We sons of Old Gent." Young Gent said defiantly.

"Greetings to sons of Old Gent. I Young Dude. I not replace him, but do my best for Momma." the

 newcomer said in fluent human treespeak. "I know you will. You and the baby Blues I see there."

"We all make Momma happy. Grow to take over our sire's task." Young Gent said, feeling less angry.

As the days, moons and seasons passed, Young Gent developed a bond with Young Dude. To his delight, Sunrise's sister, whom Momma now called Phoenix, put out larger leaves each spring, determined to survive the nasty girdling root. Sunrise, and her other sister on the western property line, Sunset, rumbled encouragement to their sibling.

The following autumn, much to Young Gent's dismay, the big Maples across the street fell before the chainsaws. They wailed in protest, and Young Gent saw signs of rot originating from tornado damage a decade and a half ago.

"Nooo!" Sunrise shouted. "Not very ill! Not yet!"

"Nooooo! Arborvitae cried.

No amount of treeish protest stopped the downing of the Maples. Young Gent knew sick trees must be downed if no cure existed, but the loss of mature trees always upset everyone. Sunrise trembled with a mix of sorrow and outrage at the loss of her friends. The next spring, however, the owner of the Maples planted two young Ornamental Pears in their place.

"Greetings!" Sunrise welcomed them to the Lands upon waking from her winter slumber. The Pears chattered with excitement, and soon, the pain of losing the Maples diminished.

Momma and her spouse wrapped Christmas lights on Young Dude each winter, and ancient memory flowed though Young Gent, mixing with the current Christmas tradition. During the third season of the new Tradition, Young Gent found himself yearning to stand with the Dude, wearing lights, enjoying Momma's delightful attentions.

"You wear now," he sang. "Someday I wear, too"

"Many seasons shall pass before then," Young Dude rumbled with mirth.

Young Gent sat contentedly in his pot, growing, waiting for the time Momma might move him to a spot where he could grow and prosper like Young Dude.

One afternoon, a vicious thunderstorm rolled across the lands. The Silver Maple shrieked as one big limb snapped and swung down. Little Princess, now a happy six foot sapling, screamed as the limb struck her, topping two feet from her trim beautiful form.

"Sorry, sorry, sorry, ow ow," the Silver Maple moaned.

"Owwowwoww," the little spruce cried. "Hurt meeee!"

"Not Silver's fault," Young Gent said, but Little Princess refused to listen.

"Hurt me!" she grumbled into the network. "Ow!"

Momma and Poppa saw the damage and Poppa reassured Momma the baby possessed the capacity to regrow her lost top. Momma calmed, and reassured the distraught sapling. True to her nature, after a short time of shock, the little conifer chose a limb for a leader and over the season, lifted it to the sun, but a season passed before she forgave Silver Maple.

****

ELEVEN

When Young Gent turned five seasons old, Momma dug him and Little Gent up with gentle caring hands, and moved them to permanent sites. Little Gent settled in Momma's old round garden where Big Apple once stood, and Young Gent felt joy as Momma placed him a mere few feet uphill of his sire's place, close to Young Dude. Momma unrolled the hose and watered in both youngsters, and as she left the hose to drip into his hole, Young Gent settled, growing his roots cell by cell.

To his dismay, that season, invaders arrived to land on Young Gent and his Spruce brethren. They burrowed into the nodes at the bud roots, and sucked sap.

"Nasty parasites! They curl new boughs! Hate them!"

"Spruce gall aphids," Young Dude grumbled. "Second time these here but this time, they infect us all!"

"Will we die?" Young Gent asked.

"Momma spray me last time, but too big now. Too many of us infested. They leave soon, but lay eggs to hatch in spring."

"Hate them," Young Gent lamented, but relaxed when the weather turned cold and insect activity ceased.

That Christmas season, after Momma and her spouse struggled to wrap the Christmas lights around the Young Dude's increasing girth and height, a gentle snowfall blanketed the land. Young Gent rumbled to Young Dude.

"A season

more, you not wear lights! I wear them!"

"No," Young Dude replied. "Momma not let you wear them for a number of seasons so not to attract attention. Many cruel humans exist and might steal you from us."

"Steal?" Alarm flashed though Young Gent. "Dig me up?"

"Worse, my little friend, worse. Cut you down." Young Dude mumbled softly into the network.

"Awful!" Young Gent shivered, almost dislodging the snow from his limbs. "I grow fast and strong."

"You shall hide in my shadows until then." Young Dude said.

"Yes, stay safe." Young Gent surveyed his land, as memory a century older than he, coursed through him, overlaying the land with an ancient image that faded slowly in the twinkling lights sparking on the snow. "Grow, fast and strong, so we make Momma happy, and before she gone, we tower into sky like times of old, and protect her and our home."

Young Dude rumbled his approval. Young Gent grew swiftly, and he and Young Dude reached into the skies. Neither wore any Christmas lights the following season, much to Young Gent's disappointment.

That spring Momma examined his boughs, concern furrowing her brow.

"Momma see them!" Young Gent said to Young Dude. "Momma see nasty gall husks!"

"She sees," Young Dude agreed as Momma examined all the conifers, grumbling. She stopped, gazing up at Young Dude.

"I can't do this myself," she muttered, and walked into the house.

"Not kill parasites?" Young Gent called after her. He wanted these nasty bugs gone. All of the spruces sported the telltale curled sprouts. "We break bud soon! Bugs hurt us! Momma?"

"She can't hear us, but she knows," Young Dude assured Young Gent.

"What can she do?" Young Gent wailed, his roots shaking.

"Maybe call a tree man," Young Dude answered.

"Tree man?" Young Gent entertained ideas of a walking tree. "What he do?"

"Patience, little friend," Young Dude responded, huffing a chuckle from his stomata. Young Gent refrained from responses, but hated the sap sucking gall aphids. He wanted them gone.

"Know," Mugo responded. "Nasty larve eat me. Try to make webs in needles! Hate them! Momma spray when see them. They come back. They almost kill me, but I grow and fight, but no longer so small."

"Still small. No worry," Young Gent said. "Momma spray soon?"

"Hope so," Mugo mumbled.

A few days later, on a cool sunny day, a Tree doctor arrived with a large sprayer, and coated Young

Gent and all the spruces with insecticide. The stuff felt funny until it dried, but it killed the insect invaders before they hatched. On the next calm sunny day, Momma sprayed Mugo, swearing and cursing the parasitic beetles that laid eggs in his new growth. To both Mugo's and Momma's delight, the soapy spray worked, and Mugo settled in to grow.

"Gone! Yes!" Young Gent cried in relief and joy. "Now grow right!"

Young Gent soon forgot the parasites, when one warm morning, Momma walked over to the neighbor's, to assist them in planting a very young Hybrid Maple sapling. Carefully they pulled the little tree out of the box.

"Sun! Sun! Air!" The little one cried from wide stomata while the humans dug a big hole.

"Welcome to the Lands!" Sunrise greeted the baby. "I happy to see tree in an old friend's empty spot."

"Greetings!" Young Gent called. "Do not fear!"

"I no fear," the baby replied. "Happy happy to be out of box!"

"I Young Gent. Welcome to the Lands."

"I Flame Maple." The baby responded to treeish good manners, even as the group of humans carefully planted her in her new home. "Hello to all."

"Grip ground, grow stout and strong," Sunrise said.

"Will!" The sapling agreed. In response, for the first time in its existence, the neighbor's house responded with a ripple of delight. Young Gent's house reciprocated with a joyous stonesong. In the next yard, a striking Weeping Cherry, covered in profuse pink blooms, rumbled.

"Greetings little One! Welcome to the Lands! Greetings all my friends!"

Beside her, an old Elm and a Hickory responded.

"Spring! Welcome all!"

"Greetings!" Young Gent answered the mature trees.

"Greetings to Son of Old Gent," the Old Hickory rumbled. "You grow and prosper. Sire be proud, proud. Hellooo Young Dude! Hello all!"

"Happy Spring!" Sunrise exclaimed. "To all on the Lands!"

Treesong filled the air, and the baby Maple trilled in delight. Young Gent spent the warm spring days telling the story of himself and his lands to the newcomer, until Flame Maple asked "Why saplings in pots down there?"

"They wait for Momma and Poppa to move them." Young Gent answered, then fretted for his remaining three brothers and the young Blue Spruces in the pots.

"We fine," Big Gent, his largest sibling, assured him. "Punch past bottoms. We fine."

"Pots confine! What happen if you grow larger than the width of pot? Suffer girdling root as Phoenix endured the year my sire fell?" Young Gent asked.

Sunrise's sister rumbled with amusement at his concern.

"As long as they are removed before their trunks reach the edge of the pots, they will be fine," Phoenix said. "Momma did not know about such when she replanted me and left a curved root in the hole. The tree surgeons removed it."

"I remember!" Young Gent replied. "I was so little, but Momma worried. Your leaves were so small and we all thought you might die."

"I was not certain either, but Momma drenched my damaged side with fungicide and it helped me heal some. My leaves are strong and large again. I am stronger."

"But you have so many dead limbs!" Young Gent protested.

"They are of no consequence." Phoenix rumbled with laughter. "They not painful. The woodpeckers like them and leave the living wood alone. Have you not noticed I once again gain height?"

"Yes!" Young Gent agreed.

"Do not fret. It will be many seasons before your siblings and their companions have any danger of girdling from their pots."

Young Gent felt mollified by the Tuliptree's confidence. He drank in the sun as summer merged into autumn.

****

TWELVE

Later that fall, snow fell from grey skies. No strong winds accompanied this storm, so the wet heavy snow accumulated. Young Gent and his conifer yardmates enjoyed the early snowfall, but a number of his deciduous friends held fast to green leaves, and murmured concerns into the network. Across the street, the young Ornamental Pears clung to very green leaves, and one of them groaned under the stress. The snow deepened, bending the hapless Pear's multiple trunks outward. His yardmate, possessing a single trunk, bore the heavy mantle with less pain. Young Gent enjoyed the snows despite the weight on his springy boughs. His kind handled deep heavy snows with ease, but not so deciduous trees in leaf. The Oak next door, creaked and moaned.

"You should not be so green still. Nor you." Young Gent warned the Oak and the Silver Maple. "Leaf fall is past! Flame Maple, Little Cherry, Big Cherry, and Sunrise sleeping! You should, too!"

"I know," the Oak mumbled. "Many of us late turners just could not help taking advantage of the unusual warm Fall weather. This is a shock."

"Its soo heavy,"the Silver Maple wailed, limbs bent. The snow swirled out of the skies, burdening all the trees that dared to hang onto their green leaves.

"No hurt me again!" Little Princess wailed as the snow burdened Silver Maple's leaf laden limbs. They hung lower and lower, creaking ominously.

Young Gent's delight in the early snowfall turned to horror, as the multiple-trunked Ornamental Pear across the street split under the snows which reached depths usually seen later in the winter. Each trunk dropped to the ground with a thump. The poor tree shrieked pain into the underground tangle of roots and to the cold air.

Behind that home, an Oak split with a crack, and thudded to the ground. The Silver Maple screamed through the network, as her branches snapped under their load, missing Little Princess by inches. The Oak swayed, and a limb cracked and dropped to the ground. The semi-dwarf Apple trees' canopies sagged to the ground but they held firm. Young Gent saw Momma come out, and knock snow off the Apples, while she spoke to the big Oak.

"Stand strong, Old One, stand strong."

The Oak groaned, but Young Gent sensed his resolve not to cave in to the weight. Young Gent felt panic, not for himself but his leafy brethren. All over the Lands, he felt many drop limbs or topple under the foot of heavy snow. The ground and air reverberated with the pain and anguish of trees caught off guard by this snowstorm. The Young Dude sang softly in the light winds, in sympathy and sorrow. Young Gent tried to sing, but his very young limbs did not respond in the breezes.

The storm slowly moved out to sea, and morning brought crisp blue skies, and a stronger wind cracked ice, dislodging clumps of snow. The sun sparkled the landscape, but Young Gent worried for his deciduous yardmates burdened with the snows on their leaves. The Silver Maple bent over, looking like a Weeping Willow. Many limbs hung twisted in her canopy and lay on the ground, surrounding the diminutive Norway Spruce.

Across the street, the one Ornamental Pear lay in four sections, split down the middle by the destructive power of the early Nor'easter. The Oak next door stood strong, and slowly the snow dropped from his canopy. His green leaves looked odd in the snowscape.

"Why this happen?" Young Gent asked.

"Just a freak storm," Young Dude rumbled with assurance. "The weather can catch us all off guard sometimes. If Sunrise was awake she'd tell you about the tornado that almost killed her when she was a bit older than you. That tornado eventually killed your sire."

Young Gent quivered, an old memory flashing through his system in bits and pieces of terrible winds, shattered limbs, torrential rains. He shut his senses to the racial memories, and concentrated on the sunlight filtering past the snow and ice to touch his needles.

The winter passed uneventful. To Young Gent's dismay, the weather continued warm and snowless. He missed the cool touch of snow on his limbs, and the slow trickle of nitrogen rich snowmelt into the reach of his questing roots. Fortunately, the spring brought enough rains to compensate for the dry winter.

That summer waxed hot and dry. Young Gent worried as Momma and Poppa began moving his stout sapling brothers and their garden mates, the young Blue Spruce saplings, to their permanent spots. They moved Bizarro Gent, Tiny Gent, and most of the Blues, including the runt, Tiny Blue, leaving two of the Blues at the corners of the old garden. Dust from the dry ground carried on the light breeze. The owners stopped at Big Gent, the largest of the group.

"I can't move him," Poppa said, after attempting to dig the young Spruce up. "We're gonna just have to cut him down."

"Oh, no," Momma cried, and tears welled up in her eyes. Young Gent sensed her grief and horror at breaking a promise. Big Gent shouted from his stomata and rumbled through his roots.

"Noooo!"

Young Gent trembled, answering his brother with his own rumblings.

"No. Momma! No!"

Momma stayed silent for a few moments, as she unrolled the hose. She suddenly turned to Poppa.

"Please, we can't lose him. He's Old Gent's baby. Can't we call the tree guys to move him?"

A long silence ensued, then Poppa nodded.

"Yes, call them."

Young Gent sang sighs of relief. The tree guys came a week later, on a drizzly cool day. Their machinery rolled across the yard, and Young Gent worried for Tiny Blue, who stood by the brush pile, a mere sprig barely four feet tall, despite his age of eight years. The machine never threatened the little spruce, nor the twin Blues that stood now in their permanent spot, waiting only for Momma to remove the constraining pots.

The men dug the hole for Big Gent, who quivered with anxiety. The men used the machine to break Big

Gent free. Gentle soft drizzle fell from grey skies, covering everyone in life giving moisture. They carried him to the big hole and carefully planted him in his permanent spot. They placed stakes in the ground, tying him in place with soft nylon straps. After the Tree men left, Momma hurried out, and checked Big Gent. Young Gent sang approval to the air, and Young Dude joined him. As Momma returned to the house, she detoured to Young Gent.

"Now you and Young Dude can take over your father's job, and your brothers and the Blues will create a beautiful little conifer park in that part of the yard." Momma raised her head, her eyes locking onto his tall leader, and she smiled. "Soon, you will wear Christmas lights."

Momma turned and walked back into the house. Young Gent inhaled her carbon dioxide laden breath, and his roots drank up the moisture that seeped into the ground. His phloem brought the water and nutrients into his ten foot body. Sunrise and her sisters sang joy from their stomata, joined by the rest of the trees in Young Gent's world.

****

THIRTEEN

As Young Gent's deciduous friends leaves turned bright and colorful wth the onset of leaf fall, Momma and Poppa brought strangers to the yard. Fear touched the young Norway Spruce as talk of digging up the yard behind the house reached him. The house radiated a strange mix of anxiety and excitement, further unnerving Young Gent.

"Do we need to move the baby tree?" Momma asked, worried.

"No," the carpenter replied. "I think there is enough room for them to maneuver."

"Good," Momma said in relief. Later that day, she hung bright green tags from his branches, to remind the workmen to avoid him. She spoke to him, love in her touch. Excitement radiated from her and over the weeks, Young Gent learned Momma and Poppa planned to build a new patio and storage shed to run the back of the old house, bringing major change after many decades. Young Dude rumbled with concern.

"Big machines like the one that moved Big Gent, will come."

"Hurt us?"

"Not know, but should not."

Momma came out to take photos of the yard. Young Gent enjoyed her attention, until she eyed the Oak next door, who still clung to green leaves tinted with gold.

"You! You'd best turn and drop those leaves! Silly tree! Remember last year? A storm is coming!" Momma admonished him and the young Pear across the street whose leaves held a touch of color. She went inside.

"Do so!" Young Gent sent into the root network, "Momma like you!"

"Know," the Oak rumbled back. Over the next week, the Oak kept his word and turned his leaves from green-gold, to dusty gold, to brown. Momma nodded and praised him whenever she walked outside. The workmen visited several times as the planning stages went forth for the new project.

One sunny, warm morning, the big machine arrived to dig up the ground. Young Gent and Young Dude both exhaled sharply from their stomata at the enormous machine.

"Much bigger than one that moved Big Gent!" Young Gent cried in alarm.

"Bigger than Pool maker!" both Dwarf Apples cried in unison.

An old memory flickered through Young Gent, of rumbling roaring machinery, larger than this one, pushing over a strange concrete lodge and digging the hole for the foundation of the home next door. His fear ebbed.

Young Dude, however, felt deep unease.

"Big machine," he rumbled.

"Not bigger than machines that make house next to ours." Young Gent said. "Sire's memories show these. We ok."

The bucket broke ground behind the old house, and Young Gent understood its unease. Nothing like this ever happened to it before, not even in seasons past, when other owners added the extension off the southwest corner of the house. The machine moved effortlessly, brushing Young Gent several times but never endangering him. Momma watched like a bird over her nest, as the hole behind the old house deepened further than Young Gent's own roots.

The backhoe rumbled, yanking away the old porch and its crumbling stairs. It lifted the old asphalt walkway, strips of sod, another set of cement stairs, and the rickety retaining wall into a great pile, creating a ramp. Young Gent noted the chunks of old root that once belonged to his sire, and felt the old connections sever from the old foundation, but just as quickly, new ones formed, thanks to Sunrise's vast root network which reached deep and far across the yard.

As the machine clawed deeper into the ground, it hit the ancient stone ledge. The worker attempted to excavate the enormous rock, but only managed to lift the rear of the growling machine. The ground vibrated, and Young Gent heard the old house protest with a groan of its own. Momma and Poppy came out to watch, and Momma's calm demeanor comforted Young Gent, and he enjoyed the warm sunshine.

By late afternoon, the deep hole ran the back of the house, but the gigantic jut of ledge budged not one leaf width. Young Gent shivered, not caring for how close the bottom of the makeshift dirt ramp came to his trunk, and breathed relief through his stomata when the digging machine left the yard.

Clouds scudded ahead on the rising wind, and Young Gent knew a huge storm churned far to the south. Knowledge rolled in through the network from scared trees in the storm's path. An old memory of devastating storms returned to him. Young Gent quivered.

"Big storm! Pressure low, low! Low, like storm long long ago!"

"How know?" Young Dude exclaimed in alarm.

"Old memory from sire!" Young Gent sent the information to Young Dude through the network.

"We strong." Young Dude responded. "Grip ground. Do as Sunrise always say. Grow thick, grow stout."

The workmen arrived the following overcast windy morning, checking out the chasm behind the old house. Momma came out, and spoke with them, and Young Gent learned the canyon would become the new huge cement patio, along with a storage shed that aligned with the old extension Momma called a bathroom. He wondered how that might be, but worry about the impending cyclone ate at his heartwood.

Wind gusts buffeted the land after the men left, and Momma hurried inside. Fears throttled Young Gent, but he drew on the old wisdom his sire bequeathed to him the day of the felling. He realized his mere nine foot height posed no danger, but Big Oak, with his remaining crown of brown leaves, rocked in the rising winds.

"Hold strong!" Young Gent cried.

"Will," the Oak rumbled.

The wind screamed over the landscape, and the damages further south, to many old and young trees alike, shocked the network. Their fear, dread and agony flashed along the interconnected root system, and Young Gent screamed from his stomata along with his yardmates as the hurricane-nor'easter passed over them. The old house creaked in the fierce gusts, but Young

Gent felt no fear from the old structure, which endured many such storms in its long existence.

After the storm moved northward, Young Gent stood firm, relief in every needle of his stout body. In Young Gent's territory only Sunrise lost a dead branch, and a few others lost small limbs, but he sensed devastation that reached far and wide from the late season hurricane. He resolved to grow stout and strong, so no storm ever damaged him.

The workers returned just after sunrise, laying out wood framing in the chasm. The sun shone bright, and Young Gent's fear of the turmoil in his yard diminished. The next morning, Momma left the house, driving away in her old black Subaru car that she loved as much as she did him. The workers checked their odd frames of wood. Suddenly, Young Gent heard the unmistakable grumble of a huge vehicle. Up the road it roared, and turned into the driveway between the houses.

"Scared!" Young Gent reacted, his stomata wide open in fear. Even Young Dude rumbled his unease into the network, as a monstrous blue truck rolled down the driveway. All the trees reacted with alarm at the presence of such a huge vehicle in the yard. The old house let out a flare of anxiety, and Young Gent knew nothing this enormous ever sat on his Lands, since the day the neighbor home's owner put in the swimming pool. This machine seemed bigger than the ones in Young Gent's memory. Across the lawn the Maples both uttered exclamations.

"HUGE machine!"

The Little Apples, shivered in fear, uneasy that such machines continued to come close to them. They remembered the pool excavation that occurred when they were but tiny saplings. Flame Maple, to Young Gent's surprise, seemed unperturbed by the heavy machinery.

"See such all the time," she commented, and Young Gent remembered she came from a place which raised trees and moved them all over the Lands.

"Momma home!" Young Dude announced, relief in his tone, but as the machine lumbered up the makeshift dirt ramp, missing him by inches, Young Gent shrieked his fears to the sky.

The truck growled and shook, while a river of grey liquid stone poured into the framing, guided by the construction workers. Momma hurried out, camera in hand. As it worked, the truck inched backwards on the increasingly slippery ramp. The pouring ceased, and the truck slowly backed out. Suddenly, it lost traction, and headed straight for Young Gent! The young spruce screamed until his stomata burned. Young Dude joined him.

"Noooo!" Momma's cry joined theirs, as she ran to Young Gent, and placed herself between the monstrous truck and Young Gent.

"NO!" Young Dude cried.

"Noooooo!" Flame Maple roused, and her cry caused Sunrise to grumble in slumber.

"Momma!" Young Gent screamed, vibrating to his very roots.

"The tree is going!" the driver called out of the truck window. Momma waved her hands.

"NO! It is not!" she shouted. The truck stopped, its rear corner touching Young Gent's boughs. One of the concrete workers hurried over, and helped guide the sliding truck.

It turned painstakingly slow, its huge tire just inches from Young Gent's trunk, while it smeared wet concrete onto his boughs. Young Gent shrilled his terror until his stomata and roots hurt. Momma fretted, dancing just outside the truck's crushing reach, until the lumbering metal beast backed up the driveway. Momma spoke to the workers, her voice sharp with worry.

"Thank you for trying so hard to miss the tree. It means a lot to me."

"It has to be moved, though." the one worker said. "It is getting too hard to maneuver here with that ramp getting so slick. The truck will be back later, too"

"I understand," Momma said, and Young Gent sensed her dread. She ran to the shed, and pulled out a spade, and dug a hole in the old garden, then ran to him and tried to dig him up, all the while crying.

"They'll kill you if I can't move you!" She wept, and snipped off a few lower boughs to reveal the ground she needed to shovel. Momma attempted to dig around him, but she failed. Young Gent no longer stood at a mere three feet high with a tiny root ball. He reached nine feet into the skies, his rootball far larger than Momma's capacity to move. She cried, and Young Gent wailed in fear.

"What happen when machine returns?"

"Not know," Young Dude answered, his tone soft.

Fortunately, delays occurred, and the workers left for the day. The huge blue and white monster did not return that afternoon. Young Gent shook, scared to the middle of his heartwood. He fretted all night.

The next morning the workers returned, and Young Gent recognized the smaller red machine as one similar to the backhoe that moved his brother Big Gent to the corner of the yard the previous summer. The machine dug a hole next to Young Dude under Momma's instructions. Another landscaper took a heavy shovel, and placing it against his largest root that ran downhill, he shoved the blade into the soil, slicing the anchoring root.

"Ooowwww!" Young Gent shouted, sharp pain lancing up to his crown.

"Sorry, Sweet One, "Momma said. "It must be done."

"Be strong," Young Dude murmured. "Pain will pass."

"Much worse than when Momma move meeee!" Young Gent complained.

"Because you bigger. I experience same when moved here, much pain, but fades fast. Be strong!"

"Try," Young Gent responded, realizing his pain ebbed.

Under Momma's watchful eye, the driver dug the bucket into the ground, cutting him off from the network.

"Noooo!" he shrilled.

"You ok," Young Dude said from his stomata. "This your third move. Should be used to it."

"Nooo," Young Gent protested.

The bucket lifted Young Gent up, then placed him in a temporary hole next to Young Dude, who stood behind a black fence made of plastic fabric that ran the length of the lawn, ending just below the biggest dwarf Apple. The man then tethered Young Gent to Young Dude with a thick green rope.

"It'll be fine there until they finish the deck and we can move him back," the landscaper said to Momma. Young Gent wondered how long that might be, and learned perhaps a mooncycle at most. The wind picked up, and snow swirled gently from grey skies. The workers left, and Momma tied him with makeshift tethers as protection against strong winds. She stroked his boughs. He took comfort in her touch, breathing quickly through his stomata, as the pains receded.

"It will be ok, Baby," she said, then went back inside.

"Don't try to connect too fast," Young Dude warned. "Less hurt when they move you back."

"Not try," Young Gent murmured, feeling too shocked to attempt growing new roots to connect back into the network.

Snow fell, covering everything in a clean white blanket. Young Gent welcomed it. He felt safe snuggled beside Young Dude, and waited for the time he returned to his spot on the lawn.

The wait grew long, as men continued to work on the old house, transforming the back of the home with each long day's work. The cement truck monster lumbered back into the yard, pouring more liquid stone into hollow wooden walls, and laid down the liquid rock in slabs. Every time the truck appeared, Young Gent whistled from his stomata in terror, but the cement mixer stayed well away from him. Finally, as the cold weather cooled the shock to his root system, the blue monster finished its work, and ceased coming to the yard.

The contractors built a shelter out of blue tarp, for the stonemasons to work under during the cold weather, over the area of the big patio slated to receive new stairs and porch. Young Gent felt a natural energy, a joy, radiating from the old house, as the workmen gave it the makeover of a century, transforming its most oddball concrete protrusions to beautiful new features.

Cold winds whistled across the land as work progressed. One sunny frigid day, gale force winds ripped the blue tarp free of the northern side of the house. It flapped in the winds until the work crew arrived and took it down. The old house hummed with delight, obviously as pleased as Momma and Poppa with new stonework and new porch. Waves of energy rolled out from the concrete and stone, as if the 108-year-old house wanted every tree and home to notice it.

"House very happy. It not like animals burrowing into the foundation. Poppa mad at woodchuck digging under old porch." Young Dude rumbled with mirth. "Not happen now. Not even little mice."

Snow fell one morning. Momma walked out to Young Gent with a shovel and tossed extra snow on his roots. Warm rains soon melted it away, then frigid cold followed, and Momma fretted over Young Gent's shallow root ball. She grabbed her last bag of mulch and laid a blanket around his system, and covered that with his boughs she snipped mooncycles ago.

The weather remained dry and frigid, and Young Gent delighted in his blanket of mulch, but the dry winds sapped him of moisture. Windburn touched his needles, and he recalled his baby days when winter-burn turned him almost yellow. His leader suffered, shriveling in the dry weather, but he felt something else amiss with his top.

One cloudy morning, Young Gent sensed a big change in the atmospheric pressure, and rumblings through the network heightened his awareness. Apprehension flared, then faded, as information came in from the network. He longed for the cool moist touch of winter precipitation.

"Storm comes!" Young Gent sang softly.

"Cold! Big snow!" Young Dude added, delight in his conifer song.

"Yes!" Young Dude replied. "Big storm, full of moisture!"

The winds roared in after nightfall, bringing with it barrage of fine snow particles blanketing the Lands quickly. Snow swirled across the new concrete deck, drifting high as the night deepened. Momma appeared on the patio, camera in hand, happy about the epic snowfall, but soon disappeared into the warm house.

Young Gent delighted in the snow driven before hurricane force winds. Beside him, Young Dude rumbled with pleasure. The wind tugged at Young Gent, but snuggled against Young Dude, he never felt any danger of toppling over.

As the night deepened, so did the snows. Sound

dwindled, as the thick snowfall muffled all noises from the nearby highway and city below the hills. The storm covered the Lands in blissful, peaceful silence, broken only by the roar of its'winds. Young Gent welcomed it, as the blizzard howled, and buried half of his body in moist comforting snow.

"Happy! Feel better!" he sang, and Young Dude rumbled in agreement.

"Snow good, nourishing."

Young Gent joined Young Dude in singing their conifer song to the stormswept skies, swaying in treeish dance with the Nor'easter's roaring winds.

****

FOURTEEN

The sun rose over Lands blanketed in three feet of fresh snow. Young Gent chortled through his stomata, enjoying the cooling touch, and loving the cozy white blanket snugging in his root ball. Momma emerged from the house, and trudged through the deep snow, snapping photos.

To Young Gent's dismay, a few days later, the snow packed, and the sun and wind slowly shrunk the protective piles. The deep snows trickled into the ground during warm spells, nourishing Young Gent's beleaguered root system, but he worried what might happen when it melted away.

Over the next few days, Momma shoveled snow onto Young Gent's roots, maintaining the protective blanket strong winds and sun took from him. No contractors arrived to work on the old house, and Young Gent sensed irritation from the building, who wanted work on its roof done as much as Momma did.

The snow melted slowly, and dry, cool weather prevailed. Each day Momma took snow from the surrounding yard, and covered his root system. Young

Gent appreciated the extra care, and his root system latched onto the ground. Young Dude rumbled warning.

"Go slow. Soon they'll move you."

"Know," Young Gent retorted. "But need water and food."

"I'll help," Young Dude said, and touched his growing roots to Young Gent's assisting him. The wait grew long.

The weather warmed, and activity around the bird feeders increased with birds returning from their winter migration, joining the birds who stayed year round. Their songs filled the air as they staked out territories and called for mates. Many used him and Young Dude as perches to survey their places, and to roost at night. Rabbits scurried under Young Dude and Little Gent, prepping for the breeding season.

"No rabbits under me," Young Gent lamented on morning.

"They will, one day," Young Dude rumbled in response. "When your boughs drape to the ground as mine do."

Workers returned that day, and tore the crumbling roof from the old house. Shock and dismay radiated from the ancient stone foundation, oozing from the old hard wood.

"You want work done. Must bear pains." Young Dude rumbled at the old house. The house groaned, then its energy level dropped, even as the wind whistled through the 108-year-old naked slats.

A memory flashed through Young Gent, something dim, vague, a glimpse of his father's memory of workers covering bare roof rafters in cedar-scented slats. He knew this old home never faced full roof replacement before. Owners before now only put new on top of old. The workers skillfully applied the new roof, and in three days, they finished, leaving the old house singing with delight. No more shingles tore free in shredded bits to scatter across the neighborhood. The wind no longer whined through gaps in the lower back roof.

Half a mooncycle passed, and Momma removed the cloth tethers she placed on him the day the cement truck almost ran him over. The stone mason crew returned, this time as landscapers. They replaced lost topsoil, working their way across the yard. Young Gent watched with growing apprehension.

Once the workers finished laying topsoil, they took a special bucket, and gently dug Young Gent out of his temporary spot. As they lifted him, he screamed.

"Momma!"To his delight, she hurried from the house as if she truly heard him. The head worker operated the machine himself, and lowered Young Gent to a freshly dug hole. Careful and skilled, they packed him in under Momma's watchful eye. They blanketed him in delightful mulch, finished seeding the lawn, leaving a straw blanket over the yard. Young Gent stood; a bit shocked, very close to his original spot Momma planted him four seasons ago. Workers left, cleaning up their tools and machinery.

Momma came out, mincing on the new planted grass, and gave him water from the hose, spraying his entire body, and drenching the ground around his root ball. He soaked it all in, delighting in the moisture after the drying winds of the past winter, and the warm spring sun. Young Dude sang in the strong breeze, but Young Gent reacted with some apprehension, standing in the open with no tethers.

"May fall!!"

"No. Root ball big and heavy," Young Dude rumbled mirth. "Now sink roots deep, Young One. Follow the water. Grip the land firmly. Know you can."

"Yes! I grow," Young Gent sang, shrugging off his fear to the wind. The days passed and the new grass grew under Momma's regular watering. She drenched his roots, too. He felt vigorous and happy, and burst bud,

popping out new growth, but his leader teased him with few green needles and weak bud break. Momma cast a concerned eye to it.

"Late as usual,"

Young Dude rumbled with treeish laugher, then added. "Leader not grow. I feel wrong in leader, too."

"BUGS!" An anguished cry echoed from Little Gent nestled in the old garden. "Bugs eat my leader! Oh, no!"

Young Gent saw his brother's leader standing brown and dead, with many lower candles drooping.

"Not galls?" He queried, feeling alarm as he felt something move in his own leader. He tried to eject the invader by oozing resin, but it failed. "We must tell Momma!"

"How?" Little Gent asked.

"Different insect invaders," Young Dude grumbled with anger and dismay. "New sprout hard to grow. Let droop. Momma see."

"Yes, must make Momma see!" Young Gent agreed, and babbled to Momma every time she came to him. She looked up at him and Young Dude's leaders, looking through binoculars, her brow furrowed.

"Momma! We sick! Help us!" Young Gent blew through his stomata every time Momma appeared outside. One hot afternoon, Momma and Poppa sat out on the new deck, eating their dinner, and Momma eyed Young Dude, and Young Gent. Her voice carried across the yard.

"Something is weird up there," she commented to Poppa.

"Heat stress?"

"No, something is amiss." Momma scowled, and Young Gent felt her increasing concern. After she finished the meal, she came back outside and took photos of Young Dude, Young Gent, and Little Gent.

"Oh poor Little Gent! What is going on up there?"

"Momma know we sick!" Young Gent cried, as she photographed his shriveled leader and drooping new top growth. She hurried inside, then returned without the camera. She frowned.

"I hate bugs. Damned White Pine weevils! Where did they come from?" Momma patted Young Gent's lower boughs. "We will get this taken care of." Momma walked back into the house.

"Tree Doctor come?" Young Gent asked."I think so," Young Dude rumbled.

Two days later, the Tree Surgeon arrived early in the morning. He carefully snipped off the infected sprouts. He took a container with a long tip and pump handle attached, and gently pushed the tip into the ground under each Spruce on the land, injecting the insecticide into the roots. Momma watched, pleased and fascinated. When the Tree surgeon finished, he stopped next to Momma.

"It will take a few months, but this should kill the weevils and the spruce gall aphids, too."

"Excellent!" She replied. "That thing looks like a giant hypodermic needle!"

The Tree Surgeon chuckled.

"If any problems arise, give us a call," he said and drove off. Momma went back in the house. The following day, gentle cooling rains arrived. Young Gent eagerly took up water, sucking up the insecticide. His fear of the invaders faded, as he felt the medicine begin its job. The sun emerged between the clouds, sparkling the rain. Young Gent drank deeply the water, ingesting more medication, and soaked up the sun in treeish bliss.

"We will be all right," Young Dude rumbled through the network. "We grow strong, battle bugs, and win."

"We do!" Little Gent agreed. "Bugs hurt me, but they now die!"

"Bugs dead on me already," Big Gent said.

"They die slow on me. I choose new leaders." Young Dude said.

"You choose two again!" Young Gent responded with treeish laughter. "She not like. You must choose one!"

"I shall, in time," Young Dude returned the mirth. "You chose already, too."

"Just one! I grow fast, long, and strong." Young Gent exclaimed in delight.

"Yeesss!" Young Dude sang in response. "Many many seasons will pass, I become Old Dude."

"We grow fast and strong, make sire proud, make Momma happy!" As the rains fell under strong sunlight, refracting the light into tiny rainbows across his boughs, Young Gent held his note, vibrating his stomata. "I shall become Old Gent!"

OLD GENT

Old Gent, in 1987, tall, proud and intact. After his felling in 2004, the author and her husband kept a slice of his trunk just below the decayed part, at about 4-5 feet about ground. They counted 108 rings. A young Norway Spruce creates the inner pith which the rings encircle at that height of 4-5 feet between its sprouting and about 5 years old. After the first few years, they grow rapidly, gaining 1-2 feet in height every year. Old Gent, at the time of his felling, was estimated to be about 110-115 years old, and given a conservative sprouting date of 1895.

Old Gent, and the old house he protected, 14 years after the tornado attack. Spring 2003, a year before the snow squall tore off the big limb on his upper right. In front, Arborvitae, 17 years after his planting as a foot high sprig. In the corner, tucked by the bathroom extension, Mugo-grafted by the author's husband for a college class in 1981.

2004 brought the fateful snowsquall and its fierce winds that ripped Old Gent's upper right boughs off, revealing the extensive decay that required his felling in April 2004.

The sad day Old Gent was cut down, revealed just how extensively the damage and rot destroyed his heartwood.

BELOW: Old Gent's old house in 2013; right-before, left-after, the extensive exterior makeover.

Left in both photos-Sunrise the Tuliptree, sprouted in 1981, moved to that location in 1986.

Right in right photo -Young Gent, sprouted 2004.

Young Gent and Young Dude reach for the skies now, as if they understand their task of taking over Old Gent's tasks.

Pictured here, they enjoy a December snowfall in 2021. Young Dude sports an exceptional crop of cones, along with all of his older Norway Spruce brethren across the Lands. Young Gent has yet to produce cones.

Flame Maple in her autumn glory, with Arborvitae and Sunrise behind her in 2020.

Before the tornado in 1989 ripped him apart, Old Gent towered over 110 feet into the skies. He was an integral part of the landscape, and even now, in 2022, 18 years after his felling, he is missed.

May all who read his tale, in this reformatted updated version, understand the special nature of trees.

Rest in peace, my grand Old Gent. 1895-2004

Marie J. Spinella-Phillips

Born in 1957, in Huntington, on Long Island, Marie J. S. Phillips has been driven by an insatiable love of writing, art, and the sciences since very early childhood. Her love of animals fueled her desire to write, always appearing as stories from the non-human point of view. She invented her very first character at six years old, creating picture books with a tree as the main protagonist. She included, on the inside covers, her very own publishing logo, complete with rainbow and shining sun!

In college, she majored in Art and Earth Sciences, where inspiration fired her vivid imagination, planting the seeds for her *Furlites of Aroriel* novels, driving her into the unique and futuristic world of Fantasy/Science Fiction.

Over the years, she developed *THE FURLITES OF ARORIEL* stories and *KHAN: A MAINE COON*, as well as *THE WHITE DRAGONS OF SUVWILUR & OTHER STORIES*. She wrote during breaks at work, at night at home, in any bit of spare time she found. Buying a home and marrying her High School beau never stopped the steady, but slow evolution of her craft. Other hobbies such as showing, collecting, and customizing model horses, as well as gardening, and photography, integrated well with her drive to complete her books.

In *OLD GENT*, Marie returns to the roots of her writing life, penning this semi-fictional biography about a century-old beloved Norway Spruce tree which graced the property she and her husband bought decades ago, showing his long life, as only she can, from the tree's point of view.

Owned by four cats, three of which are Maine Coon cats, Mrs. Phillips and her husband live in the rolling hills of northwestern Connecticut.

www.ingramcontent.com/pod-product-compliance
Lightning Source LLC
Chambersburg PA
CBHW072213280526
45788CB00002B/1000